Existentialism

"Europe now philosophizes with hammer blows", **Friedrich Nietzsche** (1844–1900) prophetically wrote. One of those who hit hardest in the 20th century was Jean-Paul Sartre. His own philosophy of Existentialism has its starting-point in a statement from his best-known novel, *Nausea* (1938).

> Everything that exists is born for no reason, carries on living through weakness, and dies by accident.

Existentialism, a way of looking at experience which Sartre made famous, was the attempt to draw all possible conclusions from the fact that there is no God. "Man", he wrote in 1943, "is a useless passion". But he is also "condemned to be free".

The Early Years

Jean-Paul Sartre, the French philosopher, playwright, novelist, essayist and political activist, was born in Paris on 21 June 1905. His mother, *née* Anne-Marie Schweitzer, was 23 years old, and his father, Jean-Baptiste, the son of a country doctor, 31.

On 17 September 1906, Jean-Baptiste Sartre, a naval officer, died of a fever contracted in Cochinchina.

His widow, without means of earning her own living, had to go back to live with her family.

→**INTRODUCING** WITHDRAWN

SARTRE

PHILIP THODY & HOWARD READ

Published in the UK in 2011
by Icon Books Ltd.,
Omnibus Business Centre,
39-41 North Road, London N7 9DP
email: info@iconbooks.co.uk
www.introducingbooks.com

Sold in the UK, Europe, South Africa
and Asia by Faber and Faber Ltd.,
Bloomsbury House,
74-77 Great Russell Street,
London WC1B 3DA
or their agents

Distributed in the UK, Europe, South
Africa and Asia by TBS Ltd.,
TBS Distribution Centre,
Colchester Road, Frating Green,
Colchester CO7 7DW

This edition published in Australia
in 2011 by Allen & Unwin Pty. Ltd.,
PO Box 8500, 83 Alexander Street,
Crows Nest, NSW 2065

Previously published in the UK and
Australia in 1998 under the title
Sartre for Beginners and in 1999 under
the current title

Reprinted 2000, 2001, 2002, 2003, 2004
and 2005

This edition published in the USA
in 2011 by Totem Books
Inquiries to: Icon Books Ltd.,
Omnibus Business Centre,
39-41 North Road,
London N7 9DP, UK

Distributed to the trade in the USA
by Consortium Book Sales & Distribution
The Keg House
34 Thirteenth Avenue NE, Suite 101
Minneapolis, Minnesota 55413-1007

Distributed in Canada by
Penguin Books Canada,
90 Eglinton Avenue East, Suite 700,
Toronto, Ontario M4P 2Y3

ISBN: 978-184831-211-1

Printed by Gutenberg Press, Malta

Sartre's origins, like those of **Roland Barthes** (1915–80), are Protestant, and this might explain his sense of being an outsider in a largely Catholic France. His maternal grandfather Charles Schweitzer was uncle to the famous Bach scholar, musician, theologian and Christian missionary **Albert Schweitzer** (1875–1965).

From 1913, I practised as a missionary doctor in the hospital I founded at the jungle village of Lambaréné in Gabon, Africa.

In 1963, Sartre published a biographical essay, *Les Mots* (*Words*). It tells the story of what he presented as a lonely and unhappy childhood, isolated from other children.

In 1917, his mother remarried, choosing as her second husband an old admirer, Joseph Mancy.

We know little of this second husband, with whom Sartre did not get on, except that he had earlier not seen himself as capable of offering Anne-Marie the kind of lifestyle which he thought she deserved.

Now that I began to make a career for myself as an engineer, I proposed marriage and took Anne-Marie and her son to live with me in La Rochelle.

For the first time in his life, in La Rochelle, Sartre began to go regularly to school. Once at school, perhaps understandably, Sartre did not get on well with his fellow pupils.

I tried to buy their friendship by offering them treats paid for with money stolen from my mother's purse.

Academically, however, he had few problems, apart from a reluctance to concentrate on the mathematics which his stepfather saw as essential to the career as an engineer which he wished to see him follow. Joseph Mancy did not himself enjoy a particularly successful career and actually went bankrupt.

In 1920, Sartre returned to Paris to study first at the prestigious *lycée Henri IV*, then the *lycée Louis le Grand*, a school with a high success rate in preparing students for the competitive examinations required for entry into one of the *grandes écoles*. In 1924, he competed successfully to enter the *École Normale Supérieure*, the most famous of all French institutes of higher education for the study of literature and philosophy, and he stayed till 1928.

The principal function of the *École Normale Supérieure* was to prepare students for the competitive examination known as the *Agrégation*, the essential step in any successful teaching career in France. Candidates successful in this examination enjoy higher pay and shorter hours of work than their less well-qualified colleagues. Then, as now, all pupils in the higher forms of the *lycées* were required to study philosophy.

It is my aim to become a philosophy teacher.

After having, to everyone's surprise, failed at his first attempt at the *Agrégation de philosophie* in 1928, Sartre was more successful in 1929. He came first, followed in the competition, in second place, by Simone de Beauvoir.

The Beaver

Simone de Beauvoir (1908–86) later wrote of her feelings for Sartre at this time in the first volume of her autobiography, *Memoirs of a Dutiful Daughter* (1958).

Although Sartre and "the Beaver" (his nickname for her) never married, they would indeed become lifelong partners.

Military Service

Before Sartre could take up the teaching post to which he was now entitled, he had to do his military service. It is an indication of what the French call *la dénatalité française* (an undesirably low birth-rate) that although Sartre was virtually blind in his left eye, he was not exempted on medical grounds and was called up again at the outbreak of the Second World War in 1939. Like a million-and-a-half other French soldiers, he was taken prisoner in the summer of 1940.

Sartre was not, however, either in 1929 or in 1939, expected to be a fighting soldier, and was put into the meteorological section. By an odd coincidence, his instructor was another French philosopher whom he already knew, **Raymond Aron** (1905–83).

In a way later resumed by the remark current in intellectual circles in Paris in the 1980s, it was better to be "wrong with Sartre rather than right with Aron".

Diverging Paths to Freedom

It is interesting at this early stage to remark on the "forks" in the road that his friends and acquaintances would later take. Sartre had become a close friend of **Paul Nizan** (1905–40) at the *lycée* and the *École Normale Supérieure*. Nizan, a journalist and novelist, was killed in action near Dunkirk in 1940. Aron would become the most distinguished and successful intellectual defender of liberal capitalism.

I joined the French Communist Party but resigned in protest at Stalin's alliance with Nazi Germany in 1939.

I'm too anarchistic to join any party.

Capitalism triumphed in France and throughout the world by the 1980s. I won the argument!

French teachers working in the public sector are all civil servants who have to go where they are posted by the Ministry of Education. Although Sartre had been sent to Le Havre and Simone de Beauvoir to Marseilles, they caused great scandal among the parents of their essentially middle-class pupils by making no secret of the fact that they were living together without being married. Both were seen as eccentric and adventurous enthusiasts of jazz and the cinema.

Nausea

In 1938, Sartre published his first novel, *La Nausée* (*Nausea*), not only an immediate and enduring success, but a work which he himself saw as the best from a literary point of view. The action takes place in the late 1920s or early 30s in a French provincial seaport to which Sartre gives the name of Bouville (Mudtown). It is fairly clearly based on Le Havre where Sartre was still teaching at the time.

Its inhabitants are presented with contempt for the rich and ironic sympathy for the poor.

The novel is written in the form of a diary kept by the central character, Antoine Roquentin. He is a bachelor, lives in a hotel, and has a small private income that enables him to devote his time to writing a biography of an 18th century adventurer, Monsieur de Rollebon. Roquentin is faced with a problem.

Why is it that everything I touch, like the feelings from my own body, makes me feel sick?

The answer, he discovers, is that there is no reason for anything to exist at all.

The fact that there is no God to provide an ultimate justification for the world is the fundamental cause of Roquentin's nausea. It is this intuition of what Sartre, through the character of Roquentin, calls the "total gratuity and absurd contingency of the universe" which gives him his feeling of perpetual sickness.

Sickness, in the sense of the desire to vomit, is the product of excess. We feel sick because we have eaten or drunk too much. Roquentin feels sick because there is just too much of everything in the universe, not only all around him but also in himself. If there were a God, there would be a very good reason for the world and all there is in it to exist, because He would have made it according to His divine will.

But since there is no God, everything is characterized by the same lack of necessity, the same contingency, the basic absurdity which Roquentin feels all around him and which inspires his nausea.

Roquentin spends a good deal of his time in a café which has a juke-box with a record of Sophie Tucker singing *Some of These Days*.

One of the ways in which I find temporary respite from my nausea is by listening to this song.

For it is, he comes to realize, like all tunes, and like all mathematical concepts, free from the absurdity and nauseating superabundance of ordinary existence.

Just as a circle carries its own definition within itself, being defined as the rotation of a straight line round a fixed point, so the existence of a piece of music lies beyond the world of accidental and contingent physical existence.

If you broke the record, or tore up the score, the song would still be there. It is not like a tree or a human being, the product of the accidental coming together of a number of physical circumstances.

It is beyond existence, in the sense that nothing that happens in the ordinary world of real objects can possibly touch it.

The solution which Roquentin finds for his problem is an essentially aesthetic one. *Nausea* ends with his decision to write a book of a particular type.

It will not only be as beautiful and hard as steel, and therefore free of the nauseating sloppiness which characterizes the natural world. It will also make men feel ashamed of their existence.

The introduction of this second aim underlines the didacticism which is also a characteristic feature of all Sartre's work. He is not only a writer who explores his own anguish. He is one who wishes to inspire the same feelings of guilt and anguish in other people.

Sartre did not follow up this idea of salvation through art in any other of his major writings. It was more the didactic aspect of Roquentin's ambition that showed itself in the books written after *Nausea*. One is tempted to see in this didacticism some kind of inherited influence from his Protestant grandfather, the man who prevented Sartre from having a normal childhood, and the uncle of the Christian missionary Albert Schweitzer.

In *Nausea*, this sinfulness takes the form of believing that human beings have rights. One of the most powerful scenes in the novel is provided by Roquentin's description of his visit to the municipal art gallery in Bouville. There, as he looks at the flattering portraits of the local worthies, he is assailed by two ideas.

Fury at their conviction that their right to exist extends to that of governing society and using it to their own profit and advantage.

Disgust at the idea that these men knew nothing of the absurd contingency of the world.

This aspect of the novel gives expression to the hatred of the French middle class which increasingly came to dominate everything that Sartre thought, wrote, or tried to do.

Existentialism

Seen from outside, Sartre's early career as a student and teacher looks like the perfect integration of a highly intelligent man into a social system ideally adapted to his tastes and talents. The books to which this experience gave rise, however, expressed a perpetual revolt against the society into which he had been born and the system in which he had been educated. This can be explained by Sartre's philosophical vision of **Existentialism**, defined in his 1946 lecture, "Existentialism is a Humanism".

> Existentialism is the attempt to draw all the conclusions from a position of total atheism.

This idea, expressed in terms of the physical sensation which dominates the book, is the central theme of *Nausea*.

Socialism

The idea that there is no God runs through the whole of Sartre's work. His total indifference to Christianity is reflected in the only mention of Christ in his work: that he was a political agitator executed by the Romans. This absence of any formal rejection of the arguments in favour of Christianity is paralleled by Sartre's omission to give chapter and verse for the despicable nature of capitalism and the wickedness of the bourgeoisie. He was clearly so confident of finding readers who agreed with him on both points that he felt no need to be specific on either of them.

Isn't it obvious? The only type of economic organization desirable in the modern world is some form of socialism.

This enthusiasm for socialism also provides what is occasionally an odd bed-fellow to the fundamental pessimism which remains constant in Sartre's world view. This came out in an interview that he gave in April 1964 to Jacqueline Piatier of *Le Monde*.

The universe remains dark. We are animals struck with disaster. (*L'univers reste noir. Nous sommes des animaux sinistrés.*)

Imagination and Freedom

At the same time as Sartre was combining his career as a teacher with the beginnings of what was rapidly to become a highly successful career as a novelist, he was also working on more strictly philosophical topics, and particularly the problem of the imagination.

The first was a short study entitled *Imagination* (1936), a patient account of the views of earlier philosophers, and a longer, more ambitious and interesting book entitled *The Psychology of the Imagination* (1940). Neither of these books made the same impact as *Nausea*, the great event of the 1938 literary season in France, and classified in 1950 as one of the six best French novels of the half century.

Both books about the imagination offer an introduction to the other central idea which dominates all of Sartre's early work, that of human freedom. Not only is he the writer who gave the most moving expression in his work to the consequences of the death of God. He is also, above all else, the philosopher of human freedom.

The Proof of Freedom

For if, as he was later to argue in a long essay entitled *What is Literature?* (1947), we were programmed like a computer to react to each individual stimulus that each isolated printed word had on us, we should never be able to stand back from the text as a whole in order to see what it all meant.

It is only our ability to put a distance between ourselves and our immediate experience which enables us to understand what is going on in a text.

And if, in a more general context, we were not free to detach our minds from the immediate environment and imagine what might not be the case – something which we can obviously all do – we should not be free.

This ability to imagine what is not the case offers the definitive proof that we are not subject to the same kind of determinism which governs the behaviour and development of animals, plants and rocks. In them, what they are – their *existence* – is totally determined by their *essence*, what they are destined to become.

The acorn has no choice but to become an oak tree, the puppy to become a dog, the piece of limestone to remain a piece of limestone.

The oak tree may grow large or small according to the soil in which it is planted.

The dog obedient or unbearable, according to the way it is trained.

The piece of rock, part of a wall or a building, according to the way human beings decide to use it.

Essence and Existence

But only human beings make choices. It is in this sense that their *existence*, as Sartre puts it, *precedes their essence*. They *are*, before being adulterers, Christians, cowards, heterosexuals, conservatives or socialists.

And they are free to take on the qualities of the particular mode of being they have chosen to adopt.

In human beings, and in human beings alone, existence precedes essence. We *are*, and we are free, before we are anything else.

This idea provides a more positive counterpoint to the metaphysical despair which informs *Nausea*. Not only do we have the moral freedom which stems from the absence of any pre-existing divine or providential plan, which it is our duty to fulfil, but we are also free in a more fundamental way, because human beings alone make choices which have *moral implications*.

The Moral Value of Existence

Metaphors taken from the natural world are relatively rare in Sartre's work. Even in a literature like that of France, which has been described as both urban and urbane, he is essentially the town-dweller's rather than the countryman's writer. But there is one passage in the 1946 lecture, *Existentialism is a Humanism*, which uses the natural world to express an idea.

Values rise from our actions as partridges do from the grass beneath our feet.

Just as we cannot stop the birds flying off and upwards at our approach, so there is no way of preventing the acts which we perform from giving rise to moral values.

Bad Faith: an Intimate Story

This idea is particularly noticeable in the book which immediately followed *Nausea*, a collection of five short stories entitled *Le Mur* (*The Wall*), published in July 1939. The story entitled "Intimité" ("Intimacy"), the second longest in the book, is not only a study in values, but also an exploration of an idea which Sartre made peculiarly his own, that of *mauvaise foi*, or bad faith.

Only a being which was free, and knew that it was free, would go out of its way, as we all sometimes do, to pretend that it was not free.

This is precisely what the story's central character, a Parisian shop assistant called Lucienne Crispin, tries to do, and in a way succeeds.

She is married to a rather unsatisfactory man called Henri.

But Henriette is puzzled as to why her friend should then insist on going to a part of Paris where she knows that Henri is almost certain to see and intercept her.

Relieved of Freedom

When the inevitable happens, and the normally placid Henri seizes his erring wife by the arm, Lucienne tries to make herself go "as limp as a bag of laundry", with Henri pulling her in one direction and Henriette in the other.

We can all remember situations in which we did everything possible to try to make somebody else take our decisions for us.

Only a being which was afraid of its freedom, and of the responsibility which this freedom brings with it, would seek to behave in this way.

It is only because we know we are free, and are afraid of our freedom, that we make such efforts to avoid it, and are capable of such feelings of relief when we sometimes manage to deprive ourselves of our freedom.

The Mind in Command

Human beings, in Sartre's view, are also so constituted that it is always the mind and not the body which is in command. For it is not because Lucienne is a passionate woman, who feels frustrated at living with her semi-impotent husband Henri, that she is tempted to go off with Pierre. It is purely to flatter her vanity.

Her behaviour offers an illustration of an idea more fully developed in Sartre's best-known philosophical work, *Being and Nothingness* (1943).

There, I quote the Austrian psychoanalyst Wilhelm Stekel . . .

Every time I have been able to get to the roots of the problem of frigidity, I always found that it lay in a *conscious* choice.

What Lucienne is afraid of is that she will, if she finally goes off with Pierre, have made a choice for which she and she alone will be responsible.

She will have brought into being the values of romantic passion and justified adultery . . .

And put them in the place of the conventional standards of petit-bourgeois marital fidelity by which she had earlier tried to live.

If I let myself go sexually, I will have given even greater reality to these values, and this is something which I am not prepared to do.

What are Emotions?

The idea that the mind is always in command of the body is a constant theme in Sartre's thought. It extends to the area in which mind-body relationships are often at their most complex, that of the *emotions*. It is, for him, not by accident that the French for "to get angry" is *se mettre en colère* (to "put" or "place" oneself in anger).

Rather than being blind forces which overwhelm us by their violence, emotions are forms of behaviour which we deliberately choose to adopt.

The last and longest of the five stories in *The Wall*, "Childhood of a Leader", explores this question of "adopted behaviour".

The main character, a young French bourgeois called Lucien Fleurier, is visited by the same awareness of the world's absurdity and his own contingency as Antoine Roquentin.

But he lacks my honesty in facing up to it.

Instead, he finds his solution in the anger towards the Jews encouraged by the right-wing Fascist movements prevalent in the France of the 1930s.

Once I allow myself to be taken over by this anger, I no longer feel disturbed, unhappy and uncertain.

He feels, on the contrary, as hard and brutal as a rock, convinced not only of his right to be a leader in society but of his duty to persecute the Jews.

When in 1946 Sartre published his important book *Réflexions sur la question juive* (*Anti-Semite and Jew*), he could remind France that Lucien's case was not a simple aberration.

The Jewish Question

Marshal Pétain, the Head of State, had signed an armistice with Hitler in 1940 which allowed for one-third of France to remain unoccupied. And so, the Vichy government came into being, voted to power by a majority of 569 to 80 in the National Assembly. It brought in anti-Semitic legislation at once without waiting for the Germans' command to do so. Tens of thousands of French Jews were systematically persecuted and eventually sent off to the death camps. By their actions, the Vichy collaborationists revealed just how deep-rooted anti-Semitism was in French society.

Entire civilized nations, including France, had fallen victim to Lucien's illness, and with even greater brutality.

Sartre's views on the emotions seem more convincing when applied to the phenomenon of anti-Semitism than as a more general account of phenomena as complex as anxiety, grief, happiness, jealousy, joy, sadness, satisfaction, or the love of children.

Lucien's story is nowadays more interesting in the way it anticipates Sartre's later view, developed more particularly in *What is Literature?* (1947), that imaginative writing really comes into its own when it deals with the problems of the society in which the author himself is living.

The Experience of War

Although *Nausea* is a novel which gives a very critical account of French society, it is not one which suggests that there is anything which anyone can do about it. Sartre's change of attitude in this respect was the result of his crucial experience, in the Second World War, as a prisoner of war, and of his participation, which he never presented as being either very daring or very important, in the Resistance movement during the Nazi occupation of France. It was (he said in 1952) only in 1945 that he made the discovery which then began to dominate everything he wrote.

Society is divided into classes. It is conflict between the classes, and more particularly the have-nots and the haves, which is the motive force in human history.

> I made the discovery that literature could speak to men of their common political concerns when a Catholic priest asked me, at Christmas 1940, to write a nativity play for my fellow prisoners of war.

He composed *Bariona, or the Son of Thunder.*

It is a strange nativity play, and there are no records of any other performances, apart from the one in Stalag XII at Trier in December 1940, where Sartre was being held by the Germans after the defeat of the French armies in the early summer of that year.

The main character is a Jewish chieftain, Bariona, in Roman-occupied Palestine.

He finally decides to lead a rebellion aimed at protecting both his own baby, not yet born, and the infant Christ, against the massacres about to be organized by King Herod and the Romans.

He does so on the grounds that both his son and the infant Christ will be born free, and should therefore be given the chance to rejoice everlastingly in their existence.

The importance of "rejoicing" is not a theme repeated in the works published by Sartre in his lifetime, where the predominant atmosphere is that of inspissated gloom. Indeed, one of the most intriguing aspects of his intellectual career in the 1940s lies in the contrast between a forward-looking, optimistic vision, as we shall see, and the contention at the end of *Being and Nothingness* (1943) that "man is a useless passion".

The Absurd

Sartre was not the only French writer of the mid-20th century to show this apparent contradiction between a social philosophy of political activism and a deep metaphysical despair. **Albert Camus** (1913–60) who was until the early 1950s quite a close friend of Sartre, also took part in the Resistance movement while at the same time publishing books like *The Outsider* (1942) or *The Myth of Sisyphus* (1943) which argued that human life was fundamentally **absurd**.

Sartre and Camus were emblematic figures whose historical significance was at the time perhaps even more important than the works they published. Both expressed the essential dilemma of post-War Europe.

The Flies

Sartre's first reply was given in the first of his "optimistic" plays to be produced on the Paris stage, *The Flies*. It is based upon the legend of Orestes, the son of the Greek king Agamemnon, who returns to Argos to avenge his father's murder by killing not only the usurper Aigisthos but also his own mother Clytemnestra, who had actually murdered Agamemnon.

Sartre's play is a fairly straightforward allegory applicable to the Resistance movement of 1940–44.

Rather curiously, it escaped the German censors who allowed the play to be put on in Paris in 1943.

A Resistance Fighter

In the original play by **Aeschylus** (c. 525–456 BC), *The Oresteia* (458 BC), Orestes had no choice but to avenge his father's murder.

This enables Orestes, in *The Flies*, to become an emblematic figure for the Resistance movement, presented by Sartre as the attempt to give France back the freedom taken from her by the alliance between the Nazis and the Vichy régime.

Freedom and Self-Awareness

When Orestes, at the end of the play, refuses to feel remorse for what he has done, he becomes a hero of the movement which Sartre's more hostile critics were later to dub, rather ironically, "resistentialism".

Orestes has, in full awareness of his own freedom and responsibility, committed an act which will also bring freedom to his fellow citizens. It was this which made him so much of a hero for the young Frenchmen coming to maturity in the mid-1940s.

After the four stultifying years under the paternalistic Vichy government with its cult of national guilt and its backward-looking motto of *Travail, Famille, Patrie* . . .

. . . which replaced the outward-looking, optimistic Republican slogan of *Liberté, Égalité, Fraternité* . . .

We too wanted to feel both free and responsible.

In the immediate post-War world, Sartre told them just what they wanted to hear.

Being and Nothingness

As recently as 1943, however, Sartre had expressed very different ideas in *Being and Nothingness*. The philosophical argument put forward in its 632 closely-printed pages develops the views on liberty first set out in the 1940 work on imagination, but brings them to a very different conclusion. Human beings are still free and Sartre still presents freedom as the feature of our experience which enables us to take part in such characteristically and uniquely human activities as reading, arguing, thinking, anticipating and choosing.

But the consequences of our freedom are much more depressing than in *The Flies*, or indeed in any other of his works.

Our freedom is linked to the fact that we can never escape from our awareness of ourselves.

Inescapable Consciousness

This idea of inescapable self-awareness, which provides the tragic theme of *Being and Nothingness*, Sartre illustrates by making one of his most obviously autobiographical characters, Mathieu Delarue, in the uncompleted series of novels entitled *Les Chemins de la liberté* (1945), a man unable to get drunk.

However much alcohol I consume, I always remain conscious of what I am, and of the choices confronting me.

Because we are always aware of ourselves, and able to imagine what is not the case, we have the freedom to stand back from our situation, evaluate it, and decide what to do.

But this perpetual consciousness has considerable disadvantages.

For there is, in Sartre's view, nothing unusual about the desire of Lucien Fleurier in "Childhood of a Leader" to have the hardness and solidity of a stone.

But this, by definition, is something which we can never do.

In *Being and Nothingness*, Sartre uses a technical vocabulary which has the initial effect of making the argument of the book seem more difficult to follow than it actually is. Human consciousness is designated by the term *le pour-soi* or the "For Itself", while physical objects in the universe are part of the *en-soi*, or "In Itself".

The aim of the *pour-soi* is to remain a *pour-soi*, while at the same time becoming an *en-soi*.

What he really means is that we would all like to *be* absolutely *what we are* with the full awareness *that we are it*.

But this, Sartre argues, is something which no human being can ever possess.

Change and Inauthentic Being

As long as we are *conscious* of what we are, we can never entirely be *what* we are.

Our freedom to change, the necessary consequence of our awareness, is always there.

And this is, by definition, something which the stone, or any other physical object, cannot have.

What about animals? Are they conscious of themselves?

Nowhere in his published work does Sartre consider the question of animals. In this, he is in the tradition of the 17th century French philosopher **René Descartes** (1596–1650), for whom animals were machines.

One of the best-known passages in *Being and Nothingness* describes a café waiter who is so ill-assured of his own identity that he plays at being a café waiter. His gestures are just a little too precise, his politeness to the customer – this is in France – just a little too ingratiating, to be genuine and spontaneous.

And, in a sense, we are all like that.

Because of the awareness which we always have of ourselves, we can never be completely ourselves. We therefore play at being ourselves, which is one way – and a dishonest or "inauthentic" way – of dealing with the problem.

Problems of "Being" and "Being Aware"

Aside from the problems of terminology, there is a fundamental problem that confronts Sartre's argument. What evidence is there to support his claim that *pour-soi* longs to become *en-soi*, while retaining the perpetual self-awareness of the *pour-soi*? We can accept Sartre's view that human beings are free, in the sense he means it, but his next crucial step is harder to follow.

To Be or To Do?

The problem arises when you look for someone who is trying to be a *pour-soi* and an *en-soi* at the same time. How does Sartre's argument compare with the way in which both you yourself and other people actually behave? What you immediately notice is that the desire *to do*, which Sartre dismisses as relatively trivial, is far more important than the longing *to be*.

A man may well say that he wants to be a good golfer, or a superb pianist, or a successful lover. But this is merely a form of words.

What I really want is *to play* golf well.

To produce beautiful sounds.

To make his lover *enjoy* the sexual act as much as he does himself.

Is there any problem about **doing** and being at the same time conscious of the fact that this is what you have done? For the German philosopher **Martin Heidegger**, Sartre's "existential" predecessor, there is indeed a problem.

The Loss of Being

Sartre owes much to Heidegger (1889–1976), not least the term "nothingness", *néant*, in his title, which derives from Heidegger's *Das Nichts*. It refers to the idea that "being" is objectless and that human nature does not exist until realized by acts of free choice.

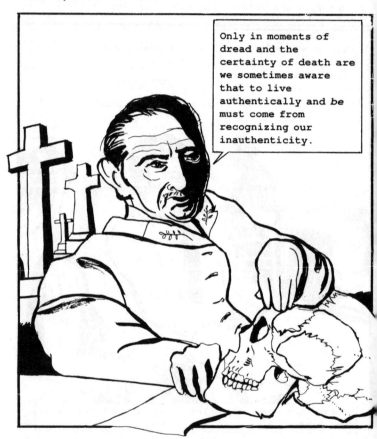

Only in moments of dread and the certainty of death are we sometimes aware that to live authentically and *be* must come from recognizing our inauthenticity.

If Sartre's terminology is difficult, it pales in comparison to Heidegger's in *Being and Time* (*Sein und Zeit*, 1927). The "problem of being" for Heidegger is that we are all concerned with the practical world of **doing**, not **being**, and thereby we "fall into inauthenticity".

We fall into the inauthenticity of what Heidegger calls "Theyness": "We take pleasure and enjoy ourselves as *they* take pleasure; we read, we see and judge about literature and art as *they* see and judge; we find shocking what *they* find shocking. The 'they', which all are, prescribes the kind of being of everydayness."

The reason why for Sartre there is no "difference" is that man can never become "God" (or *ens sui causa*: the cause of one's own being). He concludes in pessimism that inauthenticity, "theyness" and absurdity are insuperable.

No Exit

Sartre explored the theme of "theyness" by creating an "existential laboratory" in his best-known play, *Huis Clos* (*In Camera*, 1944). It was written in response to a request by three actors.

We want a play in which none of us will ever be offstage and absent from the most dramatic moments.

Each will also have the same number of lines.

And the same complexity of relationships with the other two people on stage.

The three characters in *Huis Clos* are Garcin, finally revealed as a coward, Ines, who makes no secret of being a lesbian, and Estelle, a child murderess. The hell which they inhabit is a drawing-room decorated in the style of the Second French Empire (1852–70). Their tortures are mental, not physical, and depend on a view of human relationships which Sartre derives from the German philosopher **G.W.F. Hegel** (1770–1831) who presents human minds as always in conflict with one another.

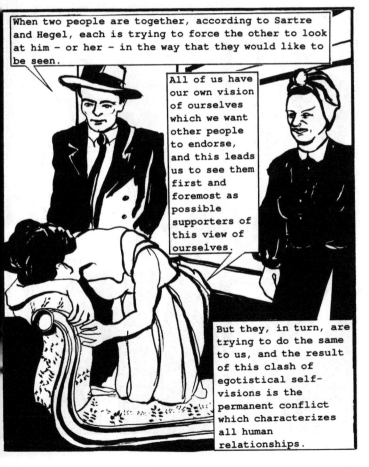

When two people are together, according to Sartre and Hegel, each is trying to force the other to look at him – or her – in the way that they would like to be seen.

All of us have our own vision of ourselves which we want other people to endorse, and this leads us to see them first and foremost as possible supporters of this view of ourselves.

But they, in turn, are trying to do the same to us, and the result of this clash of egotistical self-visions is the permanent conflict which characterizes all human relationships.

Mutual Bad Faith

It is this which leads Garcin to conclude, at the end of the play, that there is no need for the "Hellish" instruments of torture with which imaginative theologians had tried to terrify their contemporaries in earlier times.

By what Sartre presents as a process of "mutual bad faith", Garcin would persuade Estelle to see him, not as the coward that he really is . . .

But as a man who has been, unfortunately and most unfairly, let down by his body at the crucial moment.

He, in turn, would see me not as the selfish and stupid woman that I am, but as a misunderstood victim of circumstances.

But, unfortunately for both of you, Ines is here, and my critical glance destroys this mutual bad faith before it has time to establish itself.

Normally, when we are alive, we can come to terms with this struggle-to-the-death which, for Hegel and for the Sartre of *Being and Nothingness*, characterizes our relationship with other minds. So long as we are alive, we are free to alter our personality by what we do, and are not reliant solely on the way that other people look at us.

We can permanently make and remake ourselves by our acts, and thus become what our acts define us as being.

But when we are dead, the game is over, "les jeux sont faits", and we are wholly dependent upon what other people think of us.

And they will judge us solely by what we did.

This is the Hell of "theyness" – No Exit!

It is this idea, rather than Sartre's debt to Hegel's view that each mind always and at all times seeks the death of the other, which gives *In Camera* its real interest as well as its profound moral and psychological truth.

The play is dedicated "To that Lady" who once told me that she would not want to be judged by our acts.

What I think are far more important, and really make me what I am, are my intentions and my inner essence.

It is precisely this idea that Sartre is seeking to reject in his play, and there is no way in which his argument can be faulted. It is only what we *do* which defines us as human beings, just as it is a true, if melancholy fact, that other people judge us not so much on what we have done, but on what we have done wrong.

It is also hard to disagree with Sartre's view that there is no such thing as our "essential self". No man can be what Garcin claimed he was.

There is no contradiction between this and Sartre's insistence elsewhere on the idea of freedom. What Garcin did, he did freely; so that he, and he alone, was responsible for it. The ethic set out in the play is the expression of a moral attitude as austere and uncompromising as any of the principles by which Sartre's Protestant ancestors, the Schweitzers, tried to rule their lives.

In Camera has probably been performed more often, and in more different places, than any other French play written in the 20th century. In 1944, it helped to reinforce the impression that post-war French literature was as dominated by Sartre as that of the 18th century had been by his great predecessor, the Enlightenment philosopher **Voltaire** (1694–1778).

Sartre had by now been granted permanent leave from his obligations with the national education authorities to become a full-time writer. In 1945, he visited America.

My enthusiasm for the cinema led me to write an unenthusiastic account of Orson Welles's film *Citizen Kane*.

He was accompanied by one of the many mistresses against whom Simone de Beauvoir seemed to have no objection.

Sartre and Simone

Sartre and Simone de Beauvoir had a vocabulary to describe their relationship.

They rarely lived together in the same apartment or even in the same hotel. Late in 1946, after the death of Joseph Mancy in January 1945, Sartre went to live with his mother in an apartment near Saint-Germain-des-Prés, where he stayed until 1962.

Sartre's life-long association with France's best-known feminist does not seem to have much affected his male chauvinism. Critics, at the time hostile to feminism, exploited this apparent paradox, as though Simone, its most famous representative, derived all her ideas from a man. Indeed, her most influential book, *The Second Sex* (1949) does express a number of ideas also found in Sartre's work.

Women are denied their freedom by always being treated as objects in a man's world, by perpetually being placed in a situation not of their own making. They are thus denied the possibility of transcending their situation by the establishment and pursuit of projects.

Which is the way that men escape from and overcome the facticity of the natural world.

Both Sartre and Simone insisted that their ideas were developed in common, and that it is not possible to say who was the father – or mother – of the world view which she and he did so much to propagate.

Although Sartre and Simone were lovers from the early 1930s onwards, they never married, and each had what were quite often well-publicized affairs with other people. They did not have any children. In 1973, as part of her campaign in favour of the legalization of abortion in France, Simone de Beauvoir was one of the women who signed an open letter.

It stated that Sartre and I had deliberately undergone an operation to interrupt a pregnancy. We challenged the French authorities to prosecute us.

Pity that she prevented what might have been the very interesting collection of her and Sartre's genes from being passed on to the next generation. She also refused the opportunity of showing how much better she and Sartre were at bringing up children than they present their parents and grandparents as having been.

Existential Psychoanalysis of Baudelaire

In 1946, Sartre published a study of the late Romantic poet **Charles Baudelaire** (1821–67). This offers one of the best and most convincing examples of Sartre's notion of bad faith, while at the same time being the first example of the "existential psychoanalysis" which he was later to put into practice in other texts.

Existential psychoanalysis illustrates how fully Sartre differs from Freud.

It is based on the idea that the crucial age in a child's development is seven or eight, not in early infancy.

I also reject Freud's notion of the unconscious, which has no empirical foundation.

And it also differs from classic Freudian analysis both in the intensely moral tone in which Sartre writes and in his insistence on the role of *social factors* in the child's development.

Baudelaire's Case

Baudelaire was born when his father was sixty and his mother twenty-six. In 1827, when Baudelaire was six, his father died.

After a year in which I was blissfully happy as my mother's sole companion . . . she remarried!

My new husband was an intelligent and ambitious young officer, Major Aupick, eventually promoted to the rank of General.

My highly successful career ended with an appointment as French Ambassador to Constantinople.

Baudelaire was intensely jealous of him, and furious with his mother for what he saw as an act of betrayal. Indeed, so intense was his hostility towards Major Aupick that he saw him as the Laius whom he, as a new Oedipus, had to kill. Legend insists that at the time of the February 1848 revolution in Paris, Baudelaire mounted one of the barricades with the cry ...

The Classic Oedipus

Baudelaire's behaviour has led Freudian critics to see him as an almost classic case of the Oedipus complex.

He is, for the Freudian, under the influence of a set of immensely powerful, unconscious impulses which can, at best, be understood only in retrospect and as a result of a period of analysis carried out many years later.

Sartre rejects this entire Freudian notion of unconscious motives. If, in his view, we allow ourselves to be influenced by our impulses, it is because we have made a free decision to do so.

This is exactly what Baudelaire did – making the free choice to spend the whole of his life as the little boy rejected by his parents and persecuted by society.

He did so, moreover, at what Sartre sees as the crucial age of seven or eight; the age when Sartre himself made the crucial decision to become a writer which decided the course of his life, as he will report in his autobiography of 1963, *Words*.

Words and the Writer

Baudelaire was widely reviewed. Enough was known about Sartre for critics to suggest that he was to some extent projecting his own experience on to Baudelaire, while at the same time congratulating himself on not having succumbed to the temptations to which Baudelaire had too readily yielded.

In 1945, Sartre had initiated the monthly review *Les Temps Modernes*, echoing Charlie Chaplin's film *Modern Times*. In 1947, he wrote a long series of articles for the review, later published in book form, *What is Literature?*, which championed the idea of *l'écrivain engagé*, the "committed writer". The writer comes into his own only when he leaves his ivory tower to fight the good fight in the cause of progress, humanity and socialism.

Sartre's autobiography *Words* is not only a portrait of a class that he hates with an intensity which informs all his work. It is also a book with an individual villain. This is Charles Schweitzer, Sartre's grandfather.

A Difference of Choices

He read and he wrote. Indeed, he wrote so much that Charles Schweitzer, for once, behaved as Sartre thinks that normal fathers behave. Instead of playing his favourite role of adoring grandfather, and indulging in the histrionics which *Words* presents as being his normal mode of behaviour, he took the young Sartre seriously.

> With all the solemnity at his command, he warned me against the dangers of following a literary profession.

From that moment onwards, if Sartre is to be believed, the die was cast.

There is an immediate and striking difference between the intellectual atmosphere of *Words* and Sartre's account of how an orphaned child turned to literature in the study on Baudelaire. In both of them, in conformity with the concept of existential psychoanalysis set out in *Being and Nothingness*, the crucial event in their lives takes place around the age of seven.

But the presupposition is that Baudelaire always remained free to call his original choice into question, to snap out of his self-imposed role of ill-treated child and misunderstood genius. Sartre's account of his own life is quite different.

My grandfather's sudden and serious warning had the effect of making me decide to become a writer.

But although this choice then goes underground, it continues to dominate and even determine his behaviour. If, now, he writes, when he is over fifty, he is still a writer, it is to fulfil a destiny accidentally imposed by an old man on a lonely and unhappy child.

The Romantic Myth

Words is more relevant to a discussion of Baudelaire in another aspect of Sartre's argument which was, at the time, seen as even more challenging than the existential attack on Freudianism.

This was Sartre's attack on a myth which Baudelaire himself inherited from the tradition of Romanticism, and to whose strength and development he proceeded to make a major contribution.

The poet is a man perpetually doomed to solitude and unhappiness by the conflict between his own nature and that of society. By definition more noble and sensitive than other men, he is thus doomed to unhappiness by the very nature of his calling.

In Sartre's view, this myth was not only a deeply distorted account of the relationship between the writer and the society of his time.

It also offered a highly convenient way for Baudelaire to indulge in his own particular form of bad faith.

We are all tempted to run away from our freedom, but most of us do it in a less consistent and less spectacular manner.

We all try to use the circumstances of our life to make up a private myth about ourselves which absolves us from all blame . . .

While placing responsibility for what we have become on other people.

Baudelaire, as the closing sentence of Sartre's study puts it, was the prime example of this tendency: the man who had possessed the most acute awareness of human freedom, and made the greatest attempt to deny it.

Producing a Free Society

Denial of freedom was not an accusation which could, at any period in his life, have been levelled against Sartre himself. Like a large number of other writers who first became aware of politics in the 1930s, Sartre remained convinced to the end of his life that only socialism could produce a genuinely free society.

Whereas capitalism is the breeding ground for fascism, socialism aims to create a society in which everyone is free.

One of the ideas which recurs most frequently in Sartre's political writing is that no society is free unless all its members enjoy the same degree of freedom.

And since, as he argues, this is not the case in capitalist society, where members of the working class are far less free than those of the middle class – or, as he always called it, the bourgeoisie – the first task of the writer who wishes to increase human freedom is to try to produce a socialist society.

This argument, which forms the substance of the 1947 essay, *What is Literature?*, is also inseparable from the greatest problems which Sartre encountered, both as an imaginative writer and a political thinker.

For as he never ceased to insist . . .

Socialism cannot be brought about except by the working class, and cannot achieve anything unless it gives absolute priority to the needs of that class.

The Communists . . .

But in mid-20th-century France, the vast majority of the politically active working class are either paid-up members of the Communist Party . . .

Or members of the Communist-dominated trade union, *La Confédération Générale du Travail* . . .

Or people who vote regularly for Communist candidates in parliamentary elections.

Unlike Camus and George Orwell, Sartre was not prepared to wash his hands of Communism. Indeed, as late as 1961, he wrote that . . .

Whatever its crimes, the USSR has one redoubtable superiority over bourgeois democracies: it wants to bring about the revolution.

This debate with himself, as well as with his audience, about the conditions under which socialism might be achieved, inspired the 1947 play *Les Mains Sales*.

Dirtying Your Hands

Les Mains Sales – literally "dirty hands", and we shall see why – can be compared with *The Flies* of 1943. Both plots revolve around a killing and the attitude which the killer then adopts towards his act. But there is a crucial difference between Orestes in *The Flies* and the young would-be revolutionary Hugo Barine who seeks to "dirty his hands" in the 1947 play.

Indeed, it is Hugo's discovery that he committed an act of murder whose meaning he still remains free to decide, that makes the play's title *Crime Passionnel* in the English translation so appropriate.

Changes in the Communist Party Line

The crucial difference between the two plays can be appreciated if we consider the dramatic changes in the Communist "party line" between 1939 and 1947. Stalin's Russia and Hitler's Germany had signed a Non-Aggression Pact in August 1939.

And so, when Britain and France declared war against Nazi Germany on 3 September 1939, the Communist party line was to *denounce* this as an "imperialist conspiracy".

But this almost made the Communists near "allies" of the German armies occupying France since the summer of 1940!

All of this changed overnight when Nazi Germany invaded the Soviet Union on 21 June 1941.

Then, in party line support of the Soviet Union, the Communists became the implacable enemies of Nazism!

The Flies therefore celebrates that period circa 1943 when the Communists were at the forefront of the Resistance movement, and the French Communist Party for once seemed clearly and unambiguously on the side of Freedom.

But by 1947, things had changed *again*. The *Cold War* had begun . . .

The Soviet Union's occupation of Eastern Europe proved ruthless.

It was no longer axiomatic that to support Communism meant to support the "cause of freedom".

With all these extreme swings of the Communist party line policy, how should a young man like Hugo Barine *define* himself politically? This is the nub of *Les Mains Sales* . . .

The action of the play takes place during the Second World War, in an East European country to which Sartre gives the Shakespearean name of Illyria, and which is occupied by the Germans. There is a Resistance movement and the Proletarian Party is one of the most important members. The leader of its main faction is Hoederer.

Hoederer is in favour of a temporary alliance with the other, non-Communist parties in the Resistance movement.

My faction, led by Louis, is against such an alliance.

Louis' faction, in which Hugo is involved, enjoys what turns out to be the temporary support of Moscow.

In order to prevent the change of line planned by Hoederer from taking place, Hugo Barine accepts Louis' plot.

He will no longer have the feelings of uncertainty about himself and about his own identity which cause him such unhappiness. He will become, by an act which he freely commits, "the man who shot Hoederer". He will assert the values of political purity against those of opportunism and *Realpolitik* represented by Hoederer.

But Hugo is no Orestes, and Hoederer has none of the instantly recognizable villainy of Aigisthos. Indeed, it does not take long for Hugo's Hamlet-like inability to act to transform itself into affection for the man he has agreed to kill, and even into support for his policies. But Hugo has a pretty young wife, Jessica, whom he is unable to satisfy sexually, but who feels strongly attracted towards a powerful, older man.

At the very moment when Hugo comes into a room to tell Hoederer that he is going to change sides and work with him, he finds him holding Jessica in his arms. A fit of sexual jealousy enables him to do what his earlier political convictions had not been strong enough to make him do. He shoots Hoederer.

For the authorities still officially in charge in Illyria, it is a *crime passionnel*. Hugo gets two years in prison. For his erstwhile comrades in Louis' faction, it is a political murder cleverly camouflaged as a crime of sexual passion. Until, that is, new orders come from Moscow. Hoederer's policy had, after all, been the right one to pursue.

An attempt is made to murder Hugo by sending him a box of poisoned chocolates. It fails. When Hugo is released, he is still a potentially embarrassing witness whom Louis' faction would like to eliminate.

But the Party is short of members, and Hugo is given a chance to redeem himself.

If you will agree not to talk, and to see your killing of Hoederer as a purely sexual crime, you can be allowed to live and even to work again for the Party.

But Hugo, who until that moment has genuinely not really known why he killed Hoederer, suddenly makes a choice.

I now realise that I killed Hoederer for political reasons. By choosing to be killed, I will give my act the political meaning always potentially there but which I can now make explicit.

He refuses the offer to go back to the Party and is shot.

Philosophically, this is a play about freedom, identity and choice. Hugo, like the Baudelaire of Sartre's essay, is a man acutely conscious of the nature of human freedom, and equally anxious to run away from it.

I cannot come to terms with the fact that men are not like animals and physical objects – never absolutely themselves in the way that a stone or an oak tree is absolutely itself.

He cannot stand the "essence" of the human condition: the fact that we are perpetually conscious of ourselves and therefore perpetually free to become somebody different.

Just as Baudelaire succeeded, in his own eyes if not in those of Sartre, in being the incarnation of the *poète maudit* of the Romantic age, so Hugo strove to be a tough guy, a man of action, the man-who-shot-Hoederer. Hugo failed, but only partly for the reasons illustrated by the plot of *Les Mains Sales*.

For even if Hugo had, like Orestes, killed Hoederer without all the hesitations that make the play so intriguing and exciting, he would still have been in the same situation. Acts, like physical objects, do not have meaning in themselves. They have only the meaning which we remain constantly free to give them.

If Garcin had shown himself a coward but not been killed, he could still have redeemed himself on the next occasion.

But even if I had been brave then, the possibility that I might finally die a coward would still remain something I could not escape.

Even if I had decided to go back to work with the Party, this would still have remained a choice which I could call into question.

"Man", as Sartre put it in one of his strikingly memorable phrases, "is condemned to be free". There is no way, except in death, to escape from the freedom which is at the same time a blessing and a curse.

For political as much as for philosophical reasons, the production of *Les Mains Sales* in Paris on 2 April 1948 was the great event of the French theatrical season. In spite of all Sartre's protestations that he had sought merely to set out the "end/means" dilemma, and that his own preference was for the "dirty hands" approach of Hoederer rather than the idealism of Hugo . . .

The play was widely interpreted as an attack on Communism!

But what else does the plot show?

The party line is, at one and the same time, sufficiently *sacred* to justify murder, and sufficiently *flexible* to be changed at a moment's notice.

It seems to have greatly surprised Sartre that *Les Mains Sales* could be interpreted as a major contribution to the ideological crusade against the Soviet Union which was so important a feature of the Cold War.

Keeping Faith with Socialism

Indeed, in 1952, Sartre went so far as to forbid any further performances of the play. It was, he said, being taken over for purposes he had not intended and of which he did not approve. This did not prevent Sartre's criticism of the form which Communism had taken under the dictatorship of Stalin.

In 1950, he devoted a whole issue of *Les Temps Modernes* to denouncing the existence of slave labour camps in the Soviet Union.

And I was equally vigorous in my attack on Soviet repression of the movement for Hungarian independence in 1956.

But he never gave up his belief that only through the creation of socialism, and the consequent liberation of the working class, could true freedom be obtained. Only under these conditions could literature become what Sartre thought it ought to be: the self-awareness of a society in *permanent revolution*.

A difference comes over Sartre's work from 1952 onwards. His political attitudes become increasingly radical. A long series of articles began in May 1952 with the publication in *Les Temps Modernes* of "Les Communistes et la paix" (The Communists and Peace). These were sparked off by the way in which the government and right-wing press in France exploited the failure of a Communist-organized demonstration, in May 1952, against the arrival in Paris of the new NATO supreme commander, General Ridgway.

General Ridgway had served in Korea, where American, British and French troops had been joined by those of a number of other nations under the flag of the United Nations to try to repulse the invasion from the North on 24 June 1950.

The Problem of Class Awareness

Ridgway was open, in the eyes of the French Communist Party as well as in those of its many sympathizers, to the widely broadcast accusation that he had authorized the use of germ warfare against the North Koreans. The demonstration against him was, however, not a success.

Sartre saw things quite differently. For him, as he argued in "Les Communistes et la paix", the French working class achieved awareness of itself as a class only through the Communist Party. If it refused to follow the directions of the Party, it lapsed into what he was later, in *The Critique of Dialectical Reason* (1960), to call "seriality".

It becomes merely a collection of isolated individuals, equally incapable of political action and of critical self-awareness.

It was with the publication of "The Communists and Peace" that Sartre became one of the most famous of French "fellow travellers" – a sympathizer but not a Communist Party member.

The War in Indochina

Like most men and women of the left, in France and elsewhere, Sartre strongly opposed the war of 1946–54 by which France tried to hold on to her empire in Indochina (as Vietnam was then called). The French defeat at Dien-Bien-Phu in 1954 had led to the ending of this war. A temporary truce prevailed between the Communist North and the supposedly independent South, until the struggle between the two finally merged into the Vietnam War of 1965–73.

Sartre was to show even more vigour in opposing American actions in Vietnam than he had in criticizing the policies of his own government.

Cold War Attitudes

A violent opposition to what he saw as imperialist wars conducted by Western powers against the colonized peoples of the Third World remained a powerful and dominant theme in Sartre's work. He had, it is true, been slightly disturbed by the fact that the Korean War had originally broken out when heavily-armed forces from the Communist North invaded the South.

However, I explained the event as a justified response to American provocation.

And it was his hostility to the role being played by the USA in the Cold War which was a determining factor in the shift to the left which characterized his work and activity in the 1950s.

Marxism and Existentialism

Sartre continued to support the Party until the repression of the Hungarian revolt in 1956 caused him to break off all relations with it. Even then, he did not abandon his view that Marxism remained the only viable philosophy for the 20th century. It had, he admitted in an article entitled "Stalin's Ghost", in which he denounced the Soviet intervention in Hungary, been perverted by Stalinism.

But although Stalinism had been an historical necessity in the construction of socialism in the Soviet Union, this did not mean that Marxism was *wrong* or that revolutions based on Marx's ideas were doomed to failure.

It was now time for the Party to adopt more liberal policies in order to bring about genuine socialism more quickly and more efficiently. This it could do, Sartre argued in his 1957 articles in *Les Temps Modernes*, "Questions de Méthode", by accepting the kind of reform which Existentialism was capable of providing. By its attention to immediate experience, Existentialism could save Marxism from becoming a dried-out and abstract theology.

A Temporary Optimism

Marxism was the only philosophy which enabled the proletariat, the class which held the future in its hands, to make sense of its experience. But Existentialism had nonetheless a useful role to play.

The development of these views in the 1950s went hand-in-hand with the presentation of three plays, *Le Diable et le Bon Dieu* (*Lucifer and the Lord,* 1951), *Kean* (1952) and *Nekrassov* (1955), in which a succession of heroes achieved some kind of reconciliation with their fate.

Goetz, the hero of the first, gives up the attempt to achieve absolutes, in good as well as in evil.

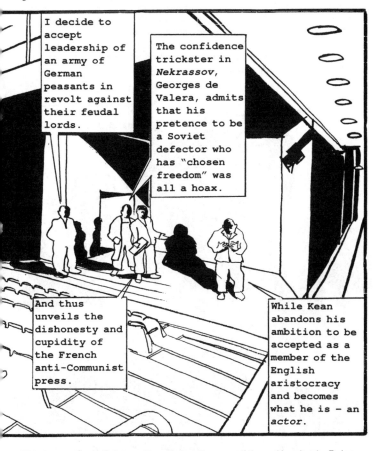

> I decide to accept leadership of an army of German peasants in revolt against their feudal lords.

> The confidence trickster in *Nekrassov*, Georges de Valera, admits that his pretence to be a Soviet defector who has "chosen freedom" was all a hoax.

> And thus unveils the dishonesty and cupidity of the French anti-Communist press.

> While Kean abandons his ambition to be accepted as a member of the English aristocracy and becomes what he is – an *actor*.

This is a particularly interesting choice, if we recall the café waiter in *Being and Nothingness,* so unsure of his identity that he "plays" at being a café waiter. In *Kean,* Sartre comes close to saying that since we have no choice but to play a role, we should do so with a conscious enthusiasm that may even give us a degree of authenticity.

On 21 August 1968, troops from the Warsaw Pact, headed by the Soviet Union, moved into Prague to crush Alexander Dubcek's version of socialism in Czechoslovakia. Sartre's reaction was one of violent but virtually nihilistic pessimism. In a preface to André Liehm's book, *Three Generations* (1970), he attacked what he saw as the establishment all over the world of a new version of the "Holy Alliance" which had repressed revolutions in Europe in the first half of the 19th century. He saw no way of repairing the inhuman machine which was now in place.

May 1968

The tragic repression of "socialism with a human face" in Czechoslovakia was a defeat which coincided almost simultaneously with the failure of the May 1968 student revolution in France. These and other defeats left Sartre in despair about the future of European politics. From the 1960s onwards, he concerned himself more with the struggles of the colonized world against their imperialist masters. How much he differed from his class and even his own family in his attitude to European imperialism is summed up in the famous remark of Dr Albert Schweitzer, the world-renowned Christian missionary and Sartre's second cousin.

The Algerian Struggle

Dr Schweitzer's paternalistic attitude was at the furthest possible remove from Sartre's view that the colonized people of Africa and Asia have both the duty and the right to shake off Western imperialism by violent revolution, as he expressed it in his preface to Frantz Fanon's *The Wretched of the Earth* (1961).

In the first stage of rebellion, killing is essential. To shoot a European is to kill two birds with one stone, eliminating an oppressor and a member of the oppressed race at one and the same time. What remains are a dead man and a free man. The survivor, for the first time, feels a national soil beneath his feet.

By the time Sartre wrote these words, the armed rebellion of the Algerian *Front de Libération Nationale* against French ownership of Algeria had been going on for seven years – beginning immediately after the French defeat in Indochina. Sartre did everything he could to prepare French public opinion to accept the fact that the idea of *L'Algérie Française* was a myth.

The sooner France gets rid of its last major colony the better.

He wrote a number of articles on the issue in *Les Temps Modernes,* and the most important of these, "Le Colonialisme est un système" (1957), is a classic account, in terms of Lenin's theory of imperialism, of how France had exploited Algeria for purely French commercial motives since the initial conquest of 1830.

It is a measure of the temperature at which political argument was conducted in France during the Algerian war (1954–62), that Sartre had to move out of his apartment after it had twice been bombed – on 19 July 1961 and 1 January 1962 – by supporters of the idea that Algeria should remain French and who objected to Sartre's participation in the campaign for its independence.

For the vast majority of men and women on the left, it was a thoroughly justified rebellion, and Sartre himself saw it as the cause of all free men.

But this liberation is something which the Algerians and the French working class have to bring about by their own efforts.

It was not something that he wanted to see the French being made to give to the Algerians by an ageing, Catholic, traditionally-minded general such as **Charles de Gaulle** (1890–1970). But this was what finally happened in 1962. The work of both Sartre and his supporters is noteworthy for the absence of any acknowledgement of what de Gaulle succeeded in doing: putting an end to the Algerian war by making Algeria an independent country, while avoiding civil war in France.

The Prisoners of Altona

In 1959, Sartre wrote what turned out to be his last major play, *Les Séquestrés d'Altona* (*Altona*), to point out to the French how disastrous the policy of *L'Algérie Française* was in political, financial, as well as moral terms.

The action of *Altona* takes place in the highly prosperous West Germany of 1959. There, in an attempt to provide some retrospective justification for his war crimes, a German officer called Franz von Gerlach has locked himself away in a garret, where he spends his time pretending that Germany is still the heap of ruins which he saw on his return from the Russian front in 1945.

A defeat of this magnitude has proved so great a disaster that anything which might have avoided it was justified.

Franz von Gerlach's father is a highly successful German ship-builder, whose business has become so large and prosperous that he can no longer exercise any control over it.

Léni is Franz's incestuous sister who loves her brother a little too much.

Double Bind

It turns out that Franz was a torturer of Russian partisans during the bitterly-fought Eastern Front campaign. He oscillates between maintaining that he is completely innocent of that crime and yet claiming that it was necessary.

> Torture was the only way I could get them to give me the information I needed to save my men from an ambush.

To the spectators in 1959, his justifications sounded very like the ones given by the Communist parties throughout the world to justify the atrocities of Stalinism. Either the reports of such crimes were all "inventions of the bourgeois press", or violence was part of all revolutions – "you can't make an omelette without breaking eggs".

When Franz is finally compelled to accept that the tortures he inflicted had served no useful purpose – and even postponed the providential defeat of Nazi Germany – he goes off to commit joint suicide with his father. They will crash their Porsche at a dangerous turning known as the Devil's Brook. He leaves behind him his last and best speech on the tape-recorder for Léni to hear.

> The beast was hiding, we surprised its glance, suddenly, in our neighbour's inner eye; then, we struck him down. Legitimate self-defence. I surprised the beast, I struck it down, a man fell, in his dying eyes I saw the beast, still alive, it was I myself. One and one make one.

Tribunal of the Crabs

It is, like his other speeches, addressed to the future, the "tribunal of crabs" envisaged as being the only creatures left alive in the 30th century, and whose impenetrable appearance symbolizes how impossible it is for us to anticipate or even understand the standards by which the future will judge our acts.

Franz recognizes, even as he makes it, how pointless his attempt is to justify in the eyes of posterity not only his own crimes but the peculiarly bloody history of the 20th century.

What Sartre wants to show is that Franz's self-justification parallels the attitude of those who support France's attempt to keep Algeria. *L'Algérie, c'est la France* – Algeria is an integral part of France, in other words.

Being required to give up Algeria would thus be as providential for France as the defeat of Hitler had proved for Germany.

Critique of Dialectical Reason

Altona is linked to other themes in Sartre's work apart from his opposition to the Algerian war. It was composed at the same time as *The Critique of Dialectical Reason* (1960), a study in philosophy and politics of comparable length and ambition to *Being and Nothingness*. The book goes far beyond Sartre's original ambition of reconciling Marxism and Existentialism and becomes a study of two major problems in political and moral philosophy.

Why is violence so universal a feature of human experience, especially in politics?

And second, what becomes of man's freedom in a world in which human beings are constantly threatened by what Sartre calls the "practico-inert" (a term which he invents in order to give a new twist to the Marxist concept of alienation)?

The Practico-Inert

The example which Sartre gives to illustrate the notion of the practico-inert is that of the Chinese peasants.

A more immediate example in Western civilization is that of the motorist caught in a series of traffic jams created by the increased availability of cars whose original intention was to enable people like himself to move about more freely. In all forms of society, human beings are increasingly, and with apparent inevitability, held prisoner by their own creations.

Capitalism, Colonialism and Violence

In *Altona*, as in *The Critique of Dialectical Reason*, it is the associated phenomena of capitalism and colonialism which are the most striking and deadly examples of the practico-inert. Just as Franz von Gerlach's father is dominated by his own business success, so also France's colony of Algeria had taken on the same role.

What began, for the colonizers of the 19th century, as a highly profitable adventure, became a millstone around the neck of 20th century France.

Critique does not suggest any solutions for the problem of the practico-inert, a concept expressed by more prosaic thinkers as the undesired and unintended consequences of human actions. At no point does Sartre say that the advent of socialism will put an end to what he presents as an inevitable law of history. The second theme in the *Critique,* the universality of violence, suggests another reason for the essentially tragic vision of history running through *Altona.* This is that all human relationships, and especially those between groups, are characterized by the phenomenon of **scarcity.**

This most frequently takes the form of the lack of enough food, clothing or money to satisfy everybody's needs. But it is also there in prosperous or apparently prosperous societies.

With us, it takes the form, for the producer, of a scarcity of customers for the over-abundance of goods produced by the economic machine, and the consequent danger of unemployment of workers in either one sector or another.

The Problem of Torture

Individual conflict was a main theme of Sartre's *Being and Nothingness* and much of his work. Now, it is also the relationships between groups which gives Sartre's analysis of the human condition a note familiar to readers of **Thomas Hobbes**'s (1588–1679) *Leviathan* (1651), with its contention that man is everywhere a wolf to man, and which highlights a peculiar feature of Sartre's work. For he is, on the one hand, a progressive and even optimistic thinker urging the belief that we are free and able to bring about a free society.

It is a contention of the *Critique* that every time we see another human being, this person appears to us as a potential rival and adversary, never as a friend. This is an idea which recurs in the closing monologue of Franz von Gerlach, the torturer.

Happy centuries, who know nothing of our hatreds, how can you understand the atrocious power of our deadly loves? One and one make one, that is the whole of our history.

The way Franz had sought to bring about his destruction of his fellow man was torture, a practice which he defines as having the aim of "transforming men into vermin during their lifetime".

Torture was widely used by the French army in its attempt to repress the Algerian movement for national independence. Again, the official statements put out by the French authorities offered two mutually contradictory explanations.

We deny that it is taking place.

On the other hand, it is the only effective riposte to the systematic campaign of urban terrorism carried out by the Algerian Liberation Front.

But that was my excuse too!

Those who protested in 1962 against Algerian independence through acts of terrorism perpetrated by the *Organisation de l'Armée Secrète* did their best to kill not only Algerians but also Frenchmen. Like Franz, the supporters of *L'Algérie Française* persisted to the end in their illusion, striving to drag France down with them in their defeat.

There are both historical and philosophical reasons why Sartre was so interested in the idea and the reality of torture. During the Second World War, when France was occupied by the Germans between 1940 and 1944, the Gestapo – aided and abetted at times by the French police – made extensive use of torture to suppress the Resistance movement. In 1945, immediately after the Liberation, Sartre explained in an article how this led everyone involved with the movement, as he was himself, constantly to ask themselves the question:

In French, the word *la question* means both a question and the institution of torture. So there was an inevitable as well as a grimly appropriate pun in the title of the book *La Question* which Henri Alleg, a member of the Communist Party and a supporter of Algerian independence, published in 1958. Sartre contributed a preface under the title of "A Victory".

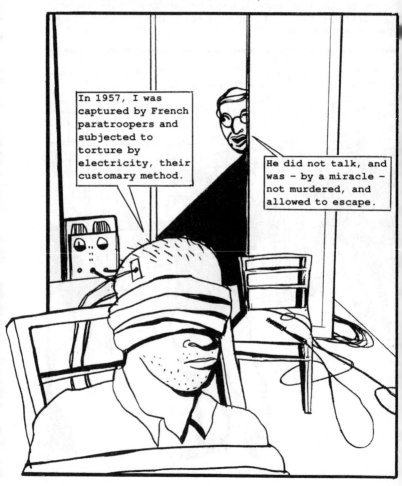

The fact that Alleg had not talked – any more than had the partisans tortured by Franz von Gerlach – provided almost a text-book illustration of one of the examples of the nature and extent of human freedom put forward in *Being and Nothingness*.

Even a man being tortured remains free, since he still retains, in his mind, the freedom to decide when or whether the moment has come at which he can bear the pain no longer.

There is a marked continuity in Sartre's thought which transcends the apparent changes which took place in the 1950s and 60s in his presentation of the nature of human freedom. To yield to your body, and to your physical fear of death and suffering, as Garcin did in *Huis Clos*, was the supreme form of bad faith. To resist, as Alleg did, the highest form of human freedom.

Saint Genet

Sartre had nevertheless seemed, from 1952 onwards, to have changed the way he thought about the existence of human freedom. That was not only the year in which he showed a greater sympathy for the essentially deterministic philosophy of Marxism, but also the year in which his second attempt at existential psychoanalysis was published, *Saint Genet, Comedian and Martyr*.

Jean Genet (1910–86) had first become known in 1942 by the semi-clandestine appearance of his first novel, *Our Lady of the Flowers*.

I wrote it in prison where I'd spent most of my life.

It appeared at first reading to glorify not only homosexuality but theft, betrayal, and the deliberate quest for evil.

Partly through the intercession of **Jean Cocteau** (1889–1963), Genet had been released from prison, and in the mid-1940s became a member of Sartre's circle of friends.

I was sufficiently impressed by his defiance of all the norms of bourgeois society to dedicate my 1947 essay on Baudelaire to him.

In 1952, Sartre's long study of Genet had officially constituted the first volume of the edition of Genet's complete works, whose publication was being undertaken by Sartre's own publisher, Gaston Gallimard.

Eight Months or Eight Years?

Nobody has ever been able to discover who Genet's father was. His mother, the unmarried Gabrielle Genet, gave birth to him in a public ward of a Paris hospital on 10 September 1910, and immediately handed him over to the public welfare authorities.

They passed me on, at the age of eight months, as a foster child to Charles and Eugénie Régnier from the agricultural area of Le Morvan, south-east of Paris.

Either because Genet deliberately misled him, or because he was so anxious to illustrate one of the basic presuppositions of existential psychoanalysis that he misheard him, Sartre wrote in *Saint Genet* that Genet had been placed as a foster child when he was *eight years old*.

Sartre also misrepresented the personality and professional status of the Régnier family, depicting them as brutal, property-obsessed peasants, when in fact Charles Régnier was a skilled artisan, and both he and his wife were very fond of children. Again, perhaps because Genet had invented a private myth about himself, Sartre also described him as having felt profoundly isolated in a society in which everybody but he himself was defined by what they owned.

This led, again according to Sartre's account in *Saint Genet*, to a "ceremony" held in the village square.

There is no independent account of such a ceremony being held, and it is not mentioned in Genet's own published works.

The ceremony is nevertheless necessary to Sartre's main thesis.

Genet decided, at that point, to take upon himself the nature of thief and evil-doer which society had forced upon him.

He took, in other words, the same kind of existentialist choice that Baudelaire had done, albeit in a way which showed, in Sartre's view, that he was more honest and authentic in his defiance of society than Baudelaire had been.

Saint Genet is a more difficult book to read than *Baudelaire*. The ambiguity of Sartre's attitude comes out when he writes that Genet had, at the age of eight, "chosen the worst", but that he had "no other choice". This is indeed true if one thinks of the impossible situation in which Genet, according to Sartre's description of his childhood, had been placed by society's attitude towards him. Indeed, part of the argument in *Saint Genet* is that capitalist society is essentially **criminogenic**.

It produces thieves and other delinquents as an inevitable consequence of its own abject nature and need for scapegoats.

Sartre's essay has remained the starting point for all studies of Genet's novels and plays. It is also, in the intellectual autobiography which Sartre provided in all his own published work, an intermediary stage between *Baudelaire* and *Words*. *Words* was also the account of a child placed in an impossible situation by the circumstances of his birth and upbringing. But the difference is crucial.

I admire Genet for the choice he made to become a criminal and to write about crime and homosexuality . . .

But I have only hatred for myself as a child and regret at the choice I made to become a writer.

Words: a Writer's Failure

It was probably by accident rather than by design that *Les Mots* (*Words*) was published in 1963, a year after the end of the Algerian war. Sartre had been working on it since 1953. He postponed publication on the grounds that it was too pessimistic.

There is no need to drag a man through the mire because he happens to write.

Since this is what the published text of *Words* tends to do – presenting Sartre's literary career as a mistake from beginning to end and pleading forgiveness rather than justification for having adopted so useless a profession – one shudders to think what the original version must have been like!

The criteria which Sartre adopts for judging his career seem rather unusual. In his interview with Jacqueline Piatier of *Le Monde* in April 1964, Sartre told her that "there is no way in which *Nausea* can outweigh a dying child" (*À côté d'un enfant qui meurt, **La Nausée** ne fait pas le poids*). He not only gives the impression of underestimating his own achievement but also of misunderstanding the whole point about writing books. For this is not to reduce world hunger. That is the job of farmers, agricultural economists and businessmen. It may well be, though the evidence for it is hard to find, that the kind of left-wing régimes to which Sartre gave his support – Communist China, Castro's Cuba, the Algeria of the FLN – have tried to cure the curse of poverty.

In that case, should not Sartre be admired for having tried to help them fight the good fight?

After all, from 1945 onwards, and his discovery of the reality of the class struggle, most of his books had tried to disturb the capitalist world order which he saw as responsible for hunger, exploitation and oppression. His books may not have succeeded. But there is no way in which he could accuse himself of not having tried.

Refusing the Nobel Prize

It was nevertheless this feeling of disillusionment with his own profession which led Sartre to become the first author, and so far the only one, to refuse the Nobel Prize for Literature when it was offered to him in October 1964. The reason officially given was that . . .

The Nobel Prize was the recognition of literary worth by an official establishment whose main concern was the maintenance of bourgeois values.

This, Sartre's admirers still maintain, was why it had been given to Albert Camus and not to André Malraux, to Anatole France and not to Marcel Proust, to François Mauriac and not to Graham Greene. The choice of Nobel laureates had always been prudent, conservative and "non-political". Sartre himself said that he would have accepted it if the prize had been offered to him during the Algerian war.

It would have been a sign of support for my opposition to the policy of *L'Algérie Française*.

But now that the war was over, it was too late.

Two Opposing Views of Literature

There were nevertheless other reasons for the intense disillusionment with literature which constitutes the leitmotif of *Words*. The first of these, if Sartre is to be believed, stems from the concept of literature inculcated in him when he was still a child by grandfather Schweitzer.

Literature is a semi-sacred activity capable of taking the place of the formal religious beliefs destroyed by the progress of science.

It was an attitude quite widespread in the France of the late 19th and early 20th centuries . . .

Committed Literature

Enough of this "salvationist" view, if *Nausea* is to be read in an autobiographical light, remained in Roquentin's view that he could attain something almost approaching salvation by writing a book.

If this was indeed what Sartre had believed at the time of writing *Nausea* in 1938, then the thesis put forward in *What is Literature?* (1947) was not simply an attack on his contemporaries.

Sartre's motive for arguing that literature should fulfil a *committed* social function was to show how wrong he had been himself in supporting the "sacred" view of literature.

But by 1963, even the belief in the efficacy of committed literature had disappeared, as the closing pages of *Words* reveal.

For a long time I looked on my pen as on a sword. Now I know how powerless we are.

All that literature can now offer, for the Sartre who presents his whole career as having been a mistake, is the chance for man to look at himself "as in a broken mirror".

It is nevertheless not only because of Sartre's rejection of two major concepts of literature that *Words* is so interesting a text. In his explanation of why he was so unhappy as a child . . .

And consequently of why I was so vulnerable to the ideas of Charles Schweitzer . . .

You come very close to rejecting the whole world view on which the philosophy of Existentialism had traditionally been based.

What was this "tradition" of Existentialism?

The First Existentialists

The basis of Existentialism is that the truth of the human condition reveals itself in moments of anguish or terror. This revelation is likely to be all the more telling and truthful if the person to whom it is vouchsafed is isolated and unusual, like the "underground man" of **Feodor Dostoievski** (1821–81), the lost, terrified heroes in the novels of **Franz Kafka** (1883–1924), or the kind of Christian held up as a model in the theology of the 17th century French philosopher and mathematician **Blaise Pascal** (1623–62) and the 19th century theologian **Søren Kierkegaard** (1813–55).

What all these thinkers have in common is not only the idea that anxiety, terror and loneliness are the natural state of man, but that anyone who seeks to escape from them is in "bad faith". We have seen strong echoes of this idea in the passage in *Nausea* in which Roquentin visits the municipal art gallery in Bouville.

What makes you so damn certain about your right to exist and possess the privileges of bourgeois society?

Similarly, the notion that there is something wrong about being integrated into the society of one's time is fundamental to Sartre's analysis of the human condition in *Being and Nothingness*.

Excluded from Normality

In *Words*, however, all this has changed. One of the most moving scenes describes how Sartre would be taken every afternoon by his mother to the Luxembourg gardens. There, ignored by the other children as they raced about in their games, they would wander from group to group.

I watched with envy the activities of my natural equals, from which it seemed that I would remain forever excluded.

But for the Existentialist, such exclusion could be nothing but a good thing.

It would have formed the natural and desirable apprenticeship for anyone who wished to write about the human condition as it really was.

The impression left by the passages describing it in *Words*, however, is totally different.

What would really have made him happy would have been to be a member of a large and vigorous family, kept in order by a father of granitic solidity, and compelled from his earliest years to learn to mix with his natural equals in the normal rough and tumble of the primary school and of children's games.

The Rough and Tumble of 1968

There was, for Sartre, as for other men and women of the left, a brief moment of optimism in the spring and summer of 1968. He fully supported the student rebellion which took place in Paris, May 1968. In 1969, after the movement had collapsed, Sartre put his name to a pamphlet entitled *The Communists are Afraid of the Revolution* in which he accused the Party of deliberately betraying the hope which the students had created of a new and genuine revolution.

The defeat of the 1968 student rebellion led to a period in which Sartre's politics became increasingly radical.

Despairing of what might be called rational politics, he supported the European Maoist movement. In 1973, he made public protests against the conditions in which the German urban terrorists known as the Baader Meinhoff gang were being held in prison.

They should be treated as revolutionaries whose protest against modern capitalist society is justified, even if their methods are not. They should not be treated as common criminals.

Voltaire in the Streets

Sartre was also vigorous in his defence of a series of newspapers put out by the extreme left, such as the Maoist-inspired *La Cause du peuple*, writing with apparent approval in 1970 that: "For the Maoists, wherever revolutionary violence stems from the masses, it is immediately and profoundly moral, for the workers, until then the victims of capitalist authoritarianism, become, if only for a moment, the subject and driving force of their own history."

In June 1970, this newspaper was banned by the police.

Sartre did continue to make a major contribution to French intellectual life in a less contentious manner. He did this not only through his books and plays but also through the monthly review, *Les Temps Modernes*, and in 1973 he helped to found the excellent left-wing daily paper *Libération*, of which he was temporarily the official editor. But the last ten years of his life, during which he was increasingly ill, witnessed a series of paradoxes.

The first of these was the way in which he shared his energy between giving his support to the most violently revolutionary movements in France and writing his fourth essay in existential psychoanalysis, the long and extremely abstruse book on **Gustave Flaubert** (1821–80), of which he published the first part in 1971 under the title *The Family Idiot*.

What was Special about Flaubert?

It is difficult, even among Sartre's greatest admirers, to find anyone who has actually read the total of 3,000 closely printed pages which make up the first three volumes. The fourth, intended to be a detailed analysis of Flaubert's great novel *Madame Bovary*, was never completed.

I said in 1979 that it was, together with *Nausea*, the best thing I had done from a purely literary point of view.

It is tempting to explain this less by the merits of the book itself and more by the role which Flaubert had played in Sartre's thinking about literature.

Words presents Flaubert as one of the authors whom the young Sartre read with the most fascination.

It was also from Flaubert's detestation of the modern world – and belief in the doctrine of life for art's sake – that Charles Schweitzer derived the concept of literature as metaphysical salvation.

And it is in its remarks about Flaubert that *What is Literature?* can be seen calling into question the view of literature which Sartre depicts as being foisted upon him in his childhood.

The Commune of 1871

Fundamental to the argument in favour of political commitment in *What is Literature?* is the view that the writer is responsible not only for the impact which his books might make, but also for the social and political events of his lifetime which might, at first sight, have nothing to do with him. For Sartre, one of the crucial events of 19th century French history was the killing of 20,000 Parisians by French government troops after the failure of the revolutionary Commune of 1871. It was this event which led Sartre to make an extreme accusation against Flaubert and the **Goncourt** brothers (**Edmond**, 1822–96 and **Jules**, 1830–70, realist novelists and art critics).

The choice both of the event and of the authors whom Sartre stigmatizes are highly significant. The repression of the Commune was directed against the Parisian working class, and both Flaubert and the Goncourt brothers were typical of the bourgeoisie whose representatives organized and endorsed the massacres.

The Family Idiot

The Family Idiot nevertheless took a different attitude towards Flaubert. He is no longer a typical representative of the class for whom Sartre felt a hatred which, as he said in 1952, would come to an end only with his death. He is, instead, an author who will be examined at greater length than Baudelaire, Genet and Sartre himself, and with a good deal more sympathy than the first, but whose career and personality are again determined by a choice which he makes between the ages of seven and nine.

There are naturally differences. Sartre, Baudelaire and Genet were all only children. Flaubert had an elder brother, Achille, a man whose intelligence made him able to become as brilliant a doctor as his father.

His success consequently blocked off any possibility that I might follow a medical career.

Gustave was also unloved by his mother who longed for a baby girl.

Add to this disadvantage the fact that Gustave is not very bright.

Words, Words, Words . . .

At the age of seven, again according to Sartre's analysis, Flaubert had not yet learned to read.

Both men, as is underlined by the title as well as the content of Sartre's 1963 autobiographical sketch, are fascinated by language, and both try to make sense of their experience by writing.

In Flaubert's case, as in Sartre's, the decision to write is a result of failure, albeit of a different kind in each case.

On the contrary, not only was Sartre a clever little boy, but one who received every encouragement to develop his talents. Flaubert, in contrast – and to sum up in nineteen words the argument of over a million – took up writing at the age of nine because he was unable to read at the age of seven.

Writing as Revolutionary Activity

Both men, in turning to literature, expressed the conflicts of their class, Flaubert without fully realizing what he was doing, Sartre with greater awareness that his aim in life was to contribute to the destruction of bourgeois civilization. He was, as can be seen, only moderately successful in this. It is an unresolved paradox that the last years of his life should have been devoted to two activities which appear so different from each other.

Read carefully, of course, *The Family Idiot* does contribute to the revolutionary project.

The real meaning of Flaubert's work, even if this was something which escaped him personally, was a diagnosis of all the contradictions of the 19th century French bourgeoisie.

But it takes a good deal of reading time, and even more reading between the lines, to see the link between this aspect of Flaubert's work and Sartre's attempt to overthrow bourgeois capitalism by lending his support to the Maoist movement in France.

Sartre, the Icon

It is indeed a strange feature of the last ten years in Sartre's life that the fewer and less accessible the books he published, the more famous he became and the more admiration he received, especially from the young. He had always been the figurehead for a political and philosophical attitude which transcended his actual published work. Let's remind ourselves of these stages in Sartre's popularity.

● In the late 1930s, *Nausea*, *Le Mur* (*The Wall*) and in 1943 *Being and Nothingness* had represented the metaphysical despair which preceded the Second World War and the Occupation of France.

● In the middle 1940s, he signalled the hopes of the Resistance movement.

● At the end of the 1940s and in the 1950s, he reflected the debates about Communism.

● In the 1960s and 1970s, he presented the totally justified revolt of the Third World peoples against Western imperialism.

● Throughout the 1970s he continued to represent the attempt to overthrow capitalism and the bourgeois state which he saw as the fundamental inspiration for May 1968, and he was widely admired for so doing. "Better", as they said in Paris at the time, "to be wrong with Sartre than right with Raymond Aron".

The Death of Sartre

Simone de Beauvoir had predicted that Sartre would never be out of her life. This did indeed prove the case, right to the very end. One of the most moving passages in the final volume of her autobiography, *La Cérémonie des Adieux* (*Adieux. A Farewell to Sartre*, 1986), is a description of Sartre's death in hospital on 15 April 1980.

I lay down for a moment by the side of his dead body, knowing that we would never meet again.

It is a measure of the success which he achieved as the standard-bearer for the cause of revolt that when he died, and his body was taken on 19 April to the Cimetière Montparnasse, the funeral procession should have been followed by a crowd of some 50,000 people.

Among the many tributes paid to Sartre after his death was that of **Valéry Giscard d'Estaing** (b. 1926), then in the sixth year of his presidency of the Fifth Republic, who described him as *une grande lueur d'intelligence* (a great light of the mind). It is doubtful whether Sartre would have paid Giscard d'Estaing as generous a tribute in comparable circumstances – but it highlights the final paradox in Sartre's life, work and ideas.

The intellectual and political freedom which he celebrated with such eloquence and conviction in the early part of his career exists most obviously not in the socialist régimes which he admired, but among the citizens of the capitalist countries which he most detested.

Notes and Further Reading

1. Sartre and Simone de Beauvoir

It is a paradox that Sartre was associated all his life with the best-known feminist in 20th century France, something which did not prevent him from being, as a creative writer, something of a male chauvinist pig (in French, *un affreux phallocrate*).

A brief review of the women in his fiction makes the point. The Marcelle of *L'Age de raison* has a clinging, leech-like passivity; Ines, in *Huis Clos*, is a total bitch, and Estelle a child murderer. Léni, in *Les Séquestrés d'Altona*, is an incestuous sister. Hilda, in *Le Diable et le Bon Dieu*, is a saintly and bossy potential leader of a troop of girl guides. And although Jessica, in *Les Mains Sales*, makes a justified protest against the way in which the men in her life treat her as a mere object, the main function given to her by Sartre in the play is to provide the excuse for Hugo to shoot Hoederer.

The only woman writer discussed by Sartre is Nathalie Sarraute, and then for only one of her novels, *Portrait d'un inconnu*. No woman forms the subject of an essay in existential psychoanalysis. Sartre shares with Freud a lack of interest in how girls come to terms with any equivalent that might exist to the Oedipus complex. No woman is treated to the kind of in-depth study which Sartre devoted in his literary essays to Georges Bataille, Maurice Blanchot, Albert Camus, John Dos Passos, William Faulkner, André Gide or Paul Nizan. At no time did he take a stand on women's rights or lend his support to campaigns in favour of birth control or abortion.

Although it is true that de Beauvoir expresses a number of ideas also found in Sartre's work, she is not simply a mouthpiece for his views. The two best books on Simone de Beauvoir are by Deirdre Blair, *Simone de Beauvoir: A Biography* (Cape, London 1990) and Toril Moy, *Simone de Beauvoir: The Making of an Intellectual Woman* (Blackwell, Oxford 1994). Toril Moy also quotes the remark which Angela Carter made in 1981: "There is one question every thinking woman in the Western world must have asked herself at one time or another. Why is a nice girl like Simone de Beauvoir sucking up to a boring old fart like Jean-Paul Sartre?"

2. Select Books by Sartre

Sartre's novels and short stories are most conveniently studied in the French 1981 *Pléiade* edition. His fiction and theatre are also widely available in paperback, in English as well as in French.

L'Imaginaire (1940) was translated in 1949 by Bernard Frechtman as *The Psychology of the Imagination*, and *L'Etre et le Néant* (1943) by Hazel Barnes as *Being and Nothingness* in 1956. Both were published by the New York Philosophical Library. *Baudelaire* (1946) was translated by Martin Turnell in 1947, and published in London by the Horizon Press and in New York by New Directions. *Saint Genet, comédien et martyr* (1952) was translated as *Saint Genet, Comedian and Martyr* by Bernard Frechtman in 1963 and published in London by W.H. Allen and New York by G. Braziller. *Les Mots* (1963) was translated by Irène Cléphane as *Words* in 1964 and published in London by Hamish Hamilton. The American translation was by Bernard Frechtman, and was published in New York by G. Braziller. *La Critique de la raison dialectique* (1960) was translated by Alan Sheridan-Smith in 1976 as *The Critique of Dialectical Reason*, and published in London by New Left Books. Volumes I, II and III of *L'Idiot de la Famille* were translated in 1982 by C. Codman as *The Family Idiot* and published by the University of Chicago Press.

3. Biographies and Bibliographies of Sartre

Bibliographical information can be found in *Sartre: Life and Works* by Kenneth and Margaret Thompson, Facts on File Publications, New York and Bicester, 1984, and in Contat and Rybalka, *The Writings of Jean-Paul Sartre*, volumes I and II, Northwestern University Press, Evanston, 1974. In addition to being a very challenging read, Andrew Dobson's *Jean-Paul Sartre and the Politics of Reason: A Theory of History*, Cambridge University Press, 1993, also contains an excellent bibliography of the very extensive published criticism of Sartre's work.

Sartre's life is best studied in Annie Cohen-Solal's *Sartre: A Life*, Heinemann, London, 1987. Cohen-Solal gives full details of the many affairs which Sartre and de Beauvoir had with other people, as Deirdre Blair and Toril Moy also do in their biographies of de Beauvoir. They name names.

4. Unfinished Works by Sartre

Sartre began a number of books which he did not complete. He did not finish a series of novels entitled *Les Chemins de la liberté*, 1945–49 (*The Paths to Freedom*), which include *L'Age de raison* (*The Age of Reason*), *Le Sursis* (*The Reprieve*) and *La Mort dans l'âme* (*Iron in the Soul*). Extracts of the fourth and final volume, *La Dernière chance* (*The Last Chance*), were published in *Les Temps Modernes* in 1949. Together with the plots of all Sartre's novels, the events of *The Last Chance* are summarized in my *Jean-Paul Sartre*, Macmillan Modern Novelists series, Macmillan, London, 1993.

Sartre did not complete *L'Idiot de la Famille*, any more than he completed the political essay *Les Communistes et la paix*, of which he published Part I in *Les Temps Modernes* in July 1952, or *La Critique de la raison dialectique* (*The Critique of Dialectical Reason*, 1960), or the essay on Tintoretto entitled *Le Prisonnier de Venise* (1957, see *Situations* VII). Neither did he ever publish the volume on ethics promised at the end of *L'Etre et le Néant* in 1943, leaving it to his literary executors to publish the *Cahiers pour une morale*, written in 1939–40, in 1983, three years after his death.

Although Sartre has generally been well served by his translators, there is something odd about the way in which certain of his titles have been put into English. In French, the phrase *l'âge de raison*, which Sartre chose as the title for the first volume of *Les Chemins de la liberté*, does not have the same meaning or associations as the term "The Age of Reason", chosen as the title for the English translation, which is normally used to designate what the French call *le siècle des lumières*, the 18th century Enlightenment. *L'âge de raison*, in contrast, refers in French to the age, between eight and nine, when a child is considered old enough to able to distinguish between right and wrong, and is therefore ready, in the Roman Catholic Church, to take her or his first communion. It is also, as will have been noticed, the critical age at which children make their basic choice in Sartre's essays in existential psychoanalysis. Since the plot of *L'Age de raison* revolves around the inability of the main character, Mathieu Delarue, to make his mind up about anything, and especially about whether or not to arrange for his mistress, Marcelle, to have an abortion or whether to marry her, the title is obviously ironic. Mathieu, who is in his mid-thirties at the time of the action of the novel, is a man who is growing old without growing up.

Le Sursis, the second volume in the "Paths to Freedom" series, describes the atmosphere in Europe at the time of the Munich crisis of September 1938. This crisis does not end in anything so permanent as a reprieve, which is the title of the English translation. It is ended by *un sursis*, the French word for a suspended sentence. The war is only postponed, and the implication of the title is that it will break out in September 1939.

An English proverb insists that it is the fool of the family who is sent into the Church. This is the implication of the title, *L'Idiot de la Famille*, which argues that Flaubert took up literature as a kind of sacred vocation because he could not do anything else; just as the younger son of an English family, whom the laws of primogeniture prevented from inheriting the estate, who was too stupid to go into medicine or the law, and not brave enough for the army, went into the Church and became a parson.

Index

Acknowledgements

Howard Read would like to thank Rupert and Helena, Kev and Alison, Gill Addison, Ann Course and Katrina Blannin.

Typesetting by **Wayzgoose**

The Authors

Philip Thody was Professor of French Literature and Head of the Department of French at the University of Leeds until his retirement in 1993. He has written studies of Barthes, Anouilh, Camus, Genet, Huxley, Proust and Sartre. He is also the author of *Introducing Barthes*.

Howard Read recently graduated from The Royal College of Art and is currently working as a freelance illustrator. In 1997, he won the student prize in the Folio Society Golden Jubilee competition.